A CourseGuide for

A Theology of Biblical Counseling

Heath Lambert

ZONDERVAN
ACADEMIC

ZONDERVAN ACADEMIC

A CourseGuide for A Theology of Biblical Counseling
Copyright © 2020 by Zondervan

Requests for information should be addressed to:
Zondervan, *3900 Sparks Dr. SE, Grand Rapids, Michigan 49546*

ISBN 978-0-310-11072-9 (softcover)

Printed in the United States of America

CONTENTS

Introduction 5

1. Counseling and Theology: A Crucial Introduction 7

2. Biblical Counseling and a Theology of Scripture 11

3. Biblical Counseling and a Theology of Common Grace 15

4. Biblical Counseling and a Theology of God. 19

5. Biblical Counseling and a Theology of Christ 23

6. Biblical Counseling and a Theology of the Holy Spirit 27

7. Biblical Counseling and a Theology of Humanity.......... 32

8. Biblical Counseling and a Theology of Sin 36

9. Biblical Counseling and a Theology of Suffering.......... 40

10. Biblical Counseling and a Theology of Salvation.......... 44

11. Biblical Counseling and a Theology of the Church......... 49

12. Biblical Counseling and the Goal of Theology 53

Introduction

Welcome to the *A CourseGuide for A Theology of Biblical Counseling*. These guides were created for formal and informal students alike who want to engage deeper in biblical, theological, or ministry studies. We hope this guide will provide an opportunity for you to grow not only in your understanding, but also in your faith.

How to Use This Guide

This guide is meant to be used in conjunction with the book *A Theology of Biblical Counseling* and its corresponding videos, *A Theology of Biblical Counseling Video Lectures*. After you have read each chapter in the book and watched the accompanying video lesson, the materials in this guide will help you review and assess what you have learned. Application-oriented questions are included as well.

Each CourseGuide has been individually designed to best equip you in your studies, but in general, you can expect the following components. Most CourseGuides begin every chapter with a "You Should Know" section, which highlights key terminology, people, and facts to remember. This section serves as a helpful summary for directing your studies. Reflection questions, typically two to three per chapter, prompt you to summarize key points you've learned. Discussion questions invite you to an even deeper level of engagement. Finally, most chapters will end with a short quiz to test your retention. You can find the answer key to each quiz at the bottom of the page following it.

For Further Study

CourseGuides accompany books and videos from some of the world's top biblical and theological scholars. They may be used independently, or in small groups or classrooms, offering quality instruction to equip students for academic and ministry pursuits. If you would like to engage in further study with Zondervan's CourseGuides, the full lineup may be viewed online. After completing your studies with *A CourseGuide for A Theology of Biblical Counseling*, we recommend moving on to *A CourseGuide for Cultural Apologetics* and *A CourseGuide for Saving Truth*.

CHAPTER 1

Counseling and Theology: A Crucial Introduction

You Should Know

- Systematic theology: what the whole Bible teaches us today about any given topic

- Good theology is concerned with: interpretation of all relevant facts in Scripture about a topic; how to place texts together; interpretation of texts in the context of the entire Bible

- Worldview: a set of beliefs about the most important issues in life

- A counselor has some sense of how to help a person move from <u>the dilemma</u> to <u>a solution</u>.

- Steps of the triple-column technique in the correct order

- Real change requires total commitment to an accurate theological vision.

- There are <u>two</u> central areas of disagreement between biblical and Christian counselors.

- There are <u>five</u> central areas of agreement between biblical and Christian counselors.

- Biblical and Christian counselors agree or disagree on a theological basis.

- The significance of Jay Adams' first book on counseling is that it illustrated how to understand counseling in relationship to Scripture.

Essay Questions

Short

1. What is required to do counseling?

2. Discuss the pros and cons of using the triple-column technique in biblical counseling. (p. 21)

3. Explain how Jay Adams' views on science affect counseling. (p. 27)

Long

1. At this point in the course, do you believe the Bible is sufficient for counseling? Or should secular techniques, science, and the Bible's teachings be combined? Explain your stance using what you've learned in this first session.

Quiz

1. (T/F) The author argues that counseling is a theological discipline.

2. What is the author's definition of counseling?
   a) Counseling is the professional provision of assistance and guidance in resolving personal, social, or psychological problems and difficulties.
   b) Counseling is a conversation where one party with questions, problems, and trouble seeks assistance from someone they believe has answers, solutions, and help.
   c) Counseling is a conversation where two parties exchange opinions and ideas before deciding an issue.
   d) Counseling is a professional relationship between one party with a problem and another party who provides advice or guidance.

3. (T/F) Good theology must be contemporary theology that provides new truths for each age.

4. (T/F) Good theology includes a recitation of what the church has believed and what the church must believe amid contemporary threats.

5. Which of the following is *not* an example of counseling?

   a) A woman contemplating divorce talking with a trained psychologist in her office
   b) A boss calls an employee into the office to discuss job performance issues
   c) A high school freshman talks with his pastor about others being mean to him at school
   d) None of the above

6. The definition of a counselee is what?

   a) Someone who has a problem and seeks help from another
   b) Someone who has a problem but doesn't want to admit the dilemma
   c) Someone who has a problem and knows what the problem is
   d) All of us are counselees and counselors at the same time

7. The twentieth-century approach to counseling was marked by which of the following?

   a) A return to the Godward nature of counseling practices
   b) A rejection of secular counseling principles by conservative Christian counselors
   c) A nearly complete rejection of God in counseling with the rise of secular practices
   d) A joining of secular and religious counseling practices into one integrated outlook

8. What is the goal of the triple-column technique in counseling?

   a) To show a counselee that automatic responses are incorrect and harmful
   b) To bring the concepts of Trinitarian theology to bear on a counselee's problem
   c) To create a workable, more biblical solution to a counselee's thoughts
   d) To create intentionality in the thinking of a counselee

9. Who laid the foundation for the modern biblical counseling movement?

   a) Jay Adams
   b) David Powlison

   c) Wayne Grudem
   d) David Burns

10. Which of the following is a main disagreement between biblical and Christian counselors?

   a) All problems are counseling problems
   b) The Bible is a sufficient resource for counseling
   c) The main motivation is the desire to offer help
   d) The helpful nature of science in counseling

CHAPTER 2

Biblical Counseling and a Theology of Scripture

You Should Know

- The authority of Scripture: The Bible is our supreme standard for what we should believe and how we should behave because it comes from God.

- The clarity of Scripture: The Holy Spirit makes the Bible understandable to all who read it seeking to be submissive to what it says.

- The necessity of Scripture: It is impossible to live the Christian life without the Bible.

- The sufficiency of Scripture: The Bible contains all that we need to know God's will and live a life pleasing to him.

- According to the author, that moment when the counselor must respond to the pain that has been revealed by a counselee is one of the most sacred occasions in all of life.

- The greatest threat today to the doctrine of the sufficiency of Scripture with regards to biblical counseling is that the Bible is not a sufficient resource to help during life's challenges.

- Good theology requires us to talk about sufficiency of Scripture in ways that are different from the Reformation era.

- Material sufficiency: The actual content of the Scripture means that the Bible tells us everything we need to know from God about any topic, can be discussed in both the general and the particular sense.

- Determining the extent of material sufficiency in a particular sense requires us to know the issue under consideration and the contents of Scripture on that issue.

- "Humble yourselves, therefore, under God's mighty hand, that he may lift you up in due time. Cast all your anxiety on him because he cares for you."—1 Peter 5:6–7

Essay Questions

Short

1. Discuss how systematic theology and the doctrine of sufficiency relates to the history of the biblical counseling movement. How do you see the sufficiency of Scripture as it relates to the biblical counseling movement of today?

2. Discuss how material sufficiency relates to biblical counseling in both the particular sense and the general sense.

3. Explain in your own words why Christian practitioners of counseling have been drawn to resources of secular therapy to augment the Bible.

Long

1. Using the example of The Westminster Confession of Faith, how would you use the sufficiency of Scripture to counsel someone with a problem? Choose an example of a personal life issue and share how you would counsel them.

Quiz

1. Which of the following are the four characteristics of Scripture?
    a) Authority, common grace, inerrancy, sufficiency
    b) Common grace, clarity, necessity, inerrancy
    c) Authority, clarity, necessity, sufficiency
    d) Omnipresence, omnisapience, omniscience, omnipotence

2. (T/F) The doctrine on which the biblical counseling movement will succeed or fail is the doctrine of sufficiency.

3. (T/F) The inerrancy of Scripture means that the Bible is completely free from error and its human authors were carried along by God and protected in their work.

4. Eric Johnson's concept of salvific doctrinal sufficiency refers to which of the following?
   a) Scripture's sufficiency only in the categories of salvation and doctrine
   b) Scripture's sufficiency only in the categories of salvation, doctrine, and counseling
   c) Scripture's sufficiency only in the categories of doctrine and the church
   d) Scripture's sufficiency in all categories

5. Today's goal of the biblical counseling movement is to defend which of the following?
   a) The necessity of Scripture in deciding biblical counseling success or failure
   b) The sufficiency of Scripture as a resource to help with life's challenges
   c) The sufficiency of Scripture in all doctrines of the church
   d) The authority of Scripture as regarding the role of the church in counseling

6. Which of the following historical examples of sufficiency does the author *not* discuss?
   a) The Reformation
   b) The First Helvetic Confession
   c) The Second Helvetic Confession
   d) The Westminster Confession of Faith

7. What are the four categories of sufficiency?
   a) Material, formal, informal, and completed
   b) Material, general, informal, and particular
   c) Progressive, completed, formal, and material
   d) Progressive, general, completed, and particular

8. Of the categories of sufficiency, which one is most disagreed upon by biblical and Christian counselors?

    a) Material
    b) Particular
    c) Progressive
    d) None of the above

9. For biblical counselors, which of the following would *not* be an objection to data from outside Scripture?

    a) The relevance of the information to biblical counseling
    b) The accuracy of the information for biblical counseling
    c) The degree to which the information encroaches on territory that belongs to ministry
    d) None of the above

10. Which of the following is a crucial difference between David in Psalm 55 and Trenyan in her case study of dealing with a painful life experience?

    a) David is honest with his pain and Trenyan is not
    b) David's pain was caused by an enemy and Trenyan's was caused by someone close to her
    c) David pours out his pain to God and Trenyan turned her pain onto herself
    d) David wants to give his situation to God and Trenyan wants to flee

CHAPTER 3

Biblical Counseling and a Theology of Common Grace

You Should Know

- The call to be a compassionate counselor requires a useful theology of biblical counseling to address both the sufficient resources for counseling within Scripture and the relevance of resources that exist outside of Scripture.

- Doctrine of common grace: the good kindness of God shown to all people regardless of whether they have experienced salvation that comes through Jesus alone

- The three different categories of common grace that God extends to us all: divine moral provision; divine physical provision; divine intellectual provision

- Common grace makes it possible for unbelievers to know facts, but the noetic effects of sin make it impossible for them to embrace the most important facts.

- "They are darkened in their understanding and separated from the life of God because of the ignorance that is in them due to the hardening of their hearts."—Ephesians 4:18

- Kuyper's observation relating science, sin, and darkened thinking: As we move from lower observation science into higher interpretation science, sin darkens our thinking most at the center of human life.

- Three levels of analysis in secular psychology: observations; interpretations; interventions

- Observations: the information all people come to know through God's common grace

- Three types of responses biblical counselors should have for using the contributions of secular psychology, as stated by the author: contributions can inform the work of biblical counseling; contributions can provoke greater faithfulness in ministering Scripture; contributions can demonstrate the effectiveness of biblical counseling

- In a biblical understanding, effective counsel always springs from a combination of an appropriate biblical strategy used by a counselor with an effective manner and received by a counselee who is willing to hear, all working under the grace of God.

Essay Questions

Short

1. Explain where the term "common grace" came from. Give some examples in your own life of God's common grace in each of the three categories of divine provision.

2. How would a biblical counselor use the three levels of analysis available in psychology?

3. Explain how the example of cognitive behavioral therapy can be an example of rejecting secular counseling techniques in biblical counseling.

Long

1. Does the refusal to incorporate secular interventions in the biblical counseling method mean a partial denial of the doctrine of common grace? Why or why not?

Quiz

1. Which of the following is *not* an example of God's common grace?

   a) God stopped the sinfulness of people in Babel by confusing their language

   b) God causes the rain to fall on the gardens of believers and unbelievers

   c) God allows evil to run rampant to its fullest potential to turn people to him

   d) God allows scientists to learn accurate information that leads to good things

2. The impact of sin on our thinking is referred to as _____.

   a) Noetic effects

   b) Common grace

   c) Secularization

   d) Darkening

3. What is the impact on counseling of the teachings found in Romans 1:18–23?

   a) God has plainly revealed himself to humanity since creation

   b) Human beings have become foolish but think they are wise

   c) Human beings suppress God's truth because of sin

   d) All of the above

4. Which of the following will best help biblical counselors distinguish between the good things resulting from God's common grace and those from the noetic effects of sin?

   a) Prayer

   b) The Bible

   c) Secular science

   d) The counselee

5. (T/F) One of the most important issues of common grace in counseling is God's intellectual provision to all people.

6. (T/F) From the beginning, the biblical counseling movement has been characterized by a complete separation from the world of secular psychology.

7. (T/F) Biblical counselors can and should be spurred by the efforts of secular psychologists to more careful biblical reflection about all counseling difficulties.

8. Which of the following is *not* given as a reason to reject secular methods of counseling while embracing common grace?

   a) Assent to false or debated information
   b) Prioritizing biblical truth over secular articulations
   c) The debate over the authority of Scripture
   d) Information that is peripheral for counseling

9. Biblical counselors emphasize the use of Scripture to the exclusion of other resources because of which of the following?

   a) A denial that accurate information is available in other places and sources
   b) A belief that the Word of God was written to offer compassionate and tangible care to his people
   c) An admission that there is nothing more important than God's common grace
   d) A confidence that science-based interventions do not stem from a true desire to help

10. Which of the following is true about cognitive behavioral therapy?

   a) All its observations are accurate representations of a counselee's problem
   b) It contains a category for an objective moral system of change
   c) It is a popular and effective way to help people change their thoughts and behavior
   d) It is an approach that has nothing in common with Scripture

ANSWER KEY
1. C, 2. A, 3. D, 4. B, 5. T, 6. F, 7. T, 8. C, 9. B, 10. C

CHAPTER 4

Biblical Counseling and a Theology of God

You Should Know

- The author refers to the doctrine of God in the context of counseling as a reference to what we know about God.

- An attribute is a quality that is true of someone and which we use to describe that person.

- God's attributes of strength: self-sufficiency, infinity, omnipresence, omniscience, omnisapience, omnipotence

- The three ways theologians often speak of God's infinity: eternality, immensity, perfection

- In the Bible, light and darkness are typically used as analogies for righteousness and sin.

- Though they are each manifestations of the kindness of God that often overlap, mercy is emphasizing God's kindness toward the needy and grace is emphasizing God's kindness toward the underserving.

- The five responses to the attributes of God for biblical counselors: be humble and engender humility in counselees; worship and lead counselees to worship; trust in God and lead counselees to trust him; orient counseling around gratitude; allow God to set the counseling agenda

- God's infinite perfection: All of God's attributes are his infinitely.

- God's attributes of care: holiness, faithfulness, goodness, love, mercy and grace, wrath

- God's holiness: his devotion to himself as God above every other reality

Essay Questions

Short

1. Why must we talk about God in biblical counseling?

2. The author states that there can be no ultimately helpful counsel that is devoid of reliance upon the self-sufficient God. Do you agree or disagree? Why?

3. Explain how the story of Joseph in Genesis affirms the work of God and men in the same action. How can you apply this concept to biblical counseling?

Long

1. Describe and explain each of the attributes of God. How would you summarize the applications of the doctrine of God in this unit for the application of biblical counseling?

Quiz

1. Regarding God, the Bible tells us which of the following?
   a) God has done many things
   b) God has motivations for his actions
   c) God wants us to know him
   d) All of the above

2. Throughout history, theologians have most commonly divided the attributes of God into which of the following categories?
   a) Moral and nonmoral attributes
   b) Absolute and relative attributes

    c) Communicable and noncommunicable attributes

    d) Strength and care attributes

3. One of the most defining features of humanity is our what?

    a) Kindness

    b) Evil sin nature

    c) "*Aseity*"

    d) Dependence

4. Which of the following do we learn about God from Acts 17:24–30?

    a) God is sufficient in himself with no needs outside of himself.

    b) The self-sufficiency of God creates our dependence on him.

    c) God demands that humans acknowledge their dependence on him.

    d) All of the above

5. Which of the following is *not* an attribute of God's strength?

    a) Self-sufficiency

    b) Faithfulness

    c) Omnisapience

    d) Infinity

6. Which of the following describes God's omnipotence?

    a) God can do anything consistent with his desires as God.

    b) God can know what is best and what to do with his wisdom.

    c) Everything God is and does is the standard for what is best.

    d) God can do anything.

7. Which attribute of God describes his complete knowledge of everything?

    a) Omnipotence

    b) Omnipresence

    c) Omniscience

    d) Omnisapience

8. Name the two obstacles biblical counselors must overcome as they gain knowledge about their counselees.

    a) Competency skills and confidence to help

    b) Competency skills and natural human limitations

   c) Natural human pride and counselee hesitation

   d) Natural human pride and wisdom to know what to say

9. Which of the following are the six attributes of God's care?

   a) Love, infinity, justice, mercy and grace, self-sufficiency, and faithfulness

   b) Honesty, goodness, faithfulness, love, holiness, and wrath

   c) Holiness, faithfulness, goodness, mercy and grace, love, and wrath

   d) Goodness, grace, faithfulness, wrath, justice, and self-sufficiency

10. The distinction between God's love and God's goodness is what?

   a) God's wisdom and God's essence

   b) God's compassion and God's omniscience

   c) God's omniscience and God's wisdom

   d) God's essence and God's compassion

CHAPTER 5

Biblical Counseling and a Theology of Christ

You Should Know

- When discussing the doctrine of Christ, it is customary to talk about the person and the work of Christ.

- The three scriptural proofs given by the author that demonstrate Jesus Christ is God: Jesus is identified as God by the authors of Scripture; Jesus is described as the creator of all; Jesus makes the actual claim that he is God

- The Council of Chalcedon first articulated the concept of hypostatic union (the biblical truth that Jesus has two natures in one person).

- "For there is one God and one mediator between God and mankind, the man Christ Jesus."—1 Timothy 2:5

- The three categories for the salvation that Jesus worked: earning our righteousness; paying sin's penalty; rising from the grave and ascending to heaven

- Peter uses the powerful language of wounds and healing to describe the work of Jesus and its effects in 1 Peter 2:24.

- The righteousness that Paul has is the righteousness that is through faith in Jesus.

- "In your relationships with one another, have the same mindset as Christ Jesus: Who, being in very nature God, did not consider equality with God something to be used to his own advantage; rather, he made himself nothing by taking the very nature of a servant, being made in human likeness. And being found in appearance as a man, he humbled himself by becoming obedient to death—even death on a cross! Therefore God exalted him to the highest place and gave him the name that is above every name."—Philippians 2:5–9

- The three things that every counselee needs the person and work of Christ for: forgiveness from sin; power to move away from sin and toward a holy life; comfort from the bitter fruits of sin

- Hebrews 7:23–25 contrasts the temporary nature of an Old Testament priest with the permanent nature of Jesus's priesthood.

Essay Questions

Short

1. Explain the two distinct natures of Jesus and why they are important. How does the difficulty of grasping Jesus's dual natures encourage you? (p. 143)

2. Why is the person of Christ inseparable from the work of Christ? (p. 145)

3. Why does Jesus's obedience only solve part of the problem we sinners have in approaching God? Why is the resurrection and ascension of Jesus an important part of what Jesus has done? (p. 148–149)

Long

1. Why is a theology of Christ important for biblical counseling? Do you agree that a theological understanding of the person and work of Jesus is *required* in counseling? Why or why not? What does the doctrine of Jesus Christ mean to you as a counselor?

Quiz

1. At the center of all truly effective counseling is _____.

   a) A true desire for helping the counselee

b) Care

c) Jesus Christ

d) The doctrine of Scripture

2. Which of the following is one of the earliest truly contentious issues about Jesus that the church confronted?

a) Jesus's humanity

b) Jesus's authenticity

c) Jesus's role in creation

d) Jesus's role in the Trinity

3. Which of the following is *not* a text in which Jesus makes a claim that he is God?

a) John 10:30

b) Matthew 26:63–64

c) Romans 9:4–5

d) John 17:5

4. Which of the following is *not* a part of the doctrine of incarnation?

a) The eternal Son of God took on flesh

b) The eternal Son of God was born of a woman

c) The eternal Son of God became a human being

d) The eternal Son of God inhabits Christians as the Holy Spirit

5. _____ is another word for the bearing of the weight of God's wrath and paying the penalty for all sin.

a) Representation

b) Propitiation

c) Mediation

d) Sanctification

6. Which of the following is the single most important distinction of Jesus's humanity from our own?

a) His conception

b) His death

c) His sinlessness

d) His divinity

7. Which of the following is not a way Jesus worked for our salvation?
    a) He showed us how to pray
    b) He paid sin's penalty
    c) He rose from the grave
    d) He earned our righteousness

8. (T/F) As sinful people, we have righteousness earned by following the law, because Jesus came to redeem us through the law.

9. (T/F) The obedience of Jesus solves only part of the problem we face as human beings and sinners who must confront a holy God.

10. The doctrine of the union with Christ teaches that _____.
    a) God bestows his grace and the comfort of his presence on those who believe
    b) When we believe in Jesus, he gives us the Holy Spirit to remain in union with himself
    c) God considers to be true of believers all that is true of Christ himself
    d) God desires to be united with us in heaven forever

CHAPTER 6

Biblical Counseling and a Theology of the Holy Spirit

You Should Know

- The Word of God is only effective when the Holy Spirit renders it effective in the lives of individuals.

- The six elements of the Holy Spirit's crucial role in counseling: convicting, indwelling, teaching, empowering, gifting, and glorifying Jesus Christ

- The function of 'sealing' is mentioned three times in the New Testament.

- The steps in order from the biblical process of determining our spiritual gifts: ask God to show me how to most fruitfully serve; consider which gifts in Scripture I desire to use in service; ask my local church leaders for guidance in discerning and using my gifts; the church provides testimony that confirms my effective use of my gift

- The first response of biblical counselors in considering all the incredible works of the Holy Spirit must be worship.

- Spirit-empowered counseling is counseling ministry based on the Word of God and Christ-centered counseling.

- The fruit of the Spirit from Galatians 5:22–23: love, joy, peace, patience, kindness, goodness, faithfulness, gentleness, self-control

- The Spirit's work of dictation: Scriptures where the Holy Spirit speaks words to people and they merely record what they have heard (Rev. 2:1 is an example)

- The Spirit's work of accommodation: the main way the Spirit authors Scripture, where the Spirit uses the unique gifts and individuality of human authors so that their personalities flow through the words of Scripture

- The reason the Spirit's work of gifting is so important in counseling: Christians have more spiritual power available to them than the power that strengthens them for Christlike obedience in their own lives (Holy Spirit empowers them for service to others)

Essay Questions

Short

1. How do you describe the importance of the Holy Spirit in a biblical approach to counseling? How do you think the Spirit's work of teaching can be used in biblical counseling?

2. How do you discover your spiritual gifts? How do you help others discover theirs? (p. 173)

3. The author gives several examples of ways to respond to the doctrine of the Spirit. Which way(s) do you typically respond to the Holy Spirit? What would trying one of these responses look like for you in a counseling situation?

Long

1. Which of the works of the Spirit do you see as the most useful in biblical counseling? Why?

Quiz

1. In John 16:8–11, the role of the Holy Spirit in the world is described in which of the following ways?
    a) Convicting the world concerning sin, righteousness, and judgment
    b) Convicting the world concerning sin, judgment, and the fruit of the Spirit

    c) Convicting the world concerning judgment, pride, and anger

    d) Convicting the world concerning sin, pride, and righteousness

2. The historical context behind the language of 'sealing' in Scripture is _____.

    a) Scribes would seal documents so that those receiving the document would know their verified authentication and could trust the contents

    b) People would be sealed into a tribe at birth, guaranteeing their belonging and acceptance

    c) A king would place his seal on a document, ensuring its safe arrival to the assigned destination

    d) Particularly important Scriptures were sealed and worn on the brow and arm as a reminder of God's commands for his people

3. The main way the Spirit authors Scripture is through the process of _____.

    a) Indwelling

    b) Accommodation

    c) Teaching

    d) Dictation

4. Which of the following is one of the central functions of the Holy Spirit?

    a) To assist believers in obeying Jesus

    b) To teach believers what passages of the Bible are most important

    c) To open the eyes of unbelievers to Jesus's love for them

    d) To enforce consequences of disobeying God's commands

5. In Galatians 5, Paul describes sin and disobedience as which of the following?

    a) Sin and disobedience

    b) Works of the flesh

    c) Teachings of the devil

    d) All of the above

6. Jesus expands on the work of the Holy Spirit in John 14:15–16 by saying _____.
   a) "All of these are empowered by one and the same Spirit, who apportions to each one individually as he wills."
   b) "You know him, for he dwells with you and will be in you."
   c) "In him you also, when you heard the word of truth, the gospel of your salvation, and believed in him, were sealed with the promised Holy Spirit, who is the guarantee of our inheritance until we acquire possession of it, to the praise of his glory."
   d) "If you love me you will keep my commandments. And I will ask the Father and he will give you another Helper to be with you forever."

7. Which of the following is the first step in a biblical process of determining individual gifts?
   a) Pray to God for direction
   b) Ask God for the gift most needed in your church
   c) Read the Bible
   d) Listen to what other church members are telling you

8. The Spirit's work is inextricably linked to which of the following:
   a) The work of God the Father
   b) The development of the church on earth
   c) The glory of Jesus Christ
   d) The revelation of biblical truths

9. The early church confirmed the deity of the Spirit at the Council of Constantinople in 381 because of which of the following:
   a) He is called God in the Bible
   b) He is listed with other members of the Trinity
   c) He does things only God can do
   d) All of the above

10. When a biblical counselor experiences failure, what should she do?
   a) Refer the counselee to someone else so the counselee may succeed
   b) Evaluate her counseling and ask God to show her areas for improvement

c) Assume her counseling practices were good and the counselee is the problem

d) Take more biblical counseling classes to better learn how to solve the problem

CHAPTER 7

Biblical Counseling and a Theology of Humanity

You Should Know

- The biblical nature of what it means to be a human being: the doctrine of humanity

- Three ways that human beings manifest the image of God to uniquely represent him in the world: who we are (cognitive reasoning abilities, our moral life); our relationships (with God and with others); what we do (dominion over creation)

- As with all the ways in which we image God, our care for the world is greatly diminished from God's unmatched power and unfading goodness.

- Even in a fallen world, the image of God in man is the foundation for the sanctity of human life.

- The goal of counseling should be to facilitate the restoration of the image of God to its proper functioning in all the practical ways that it has been shattered in the lives of those who come to see a counselor.

- The four significant terms used in the Bible to indicate the existence of an immaterial soul: soul, spirit, hidden person, and inner self

- Edward Welch argues that in a biblical theology of humanity, we must understand the heart as the "initiator" of moral action and the body as the "mediator" of moral action.

- Evangelical feminism, or egalitarianism: Christians who argue that there is no difference between the sexes in the roles they are to carry out (Galatians 3:28–all distinctions removed by Christ)

- Men are called to a position of spiritual leadership in the church, and women are called to respond to this leadership.

- "Intersex": a physical condition where the normal biological indicators of gender are confused, making it challenging to identify whether one is a boy or a girl

Essay Questions

Short

1. Explain how we are like God and portray his nature to the world in your own words. How does the doctrine of the image of God affect biblical counseling?

2. Describe the four implications of human beings having both a body and a soul for biblical counseling in your own words.

3. How do you explain the ideas that men and women are both equal and different? Discuss how the concepts of manhood and womanhood can present issues in marriage counseling.

Long

1. Which of the three categories that the author discusses within the doctrine of humanity (made in God's image, made with a body and soul, and made male and female) do you see as the most important for biblical counseling? Explain how you would council someone struggling with sin's consequences using this aspect of humanity.

Quiz

1. Which of the following is *not* typically addressed when Christians address the theology of humanity?

    a) The design of man as God's image bearer
    b) The essence and nature of mankind

c) The past and future of mankind's relationship with God

d) The issues of gender and human sexuality

2. Which of the following is a true statement about who we are?

   a) Being made in the image of God means that we are identical to God.

   b) Being made in the image of God requires that we resemble him enough to portray who he is to the rest of the world.

   c) Being made in the image of God means that we must worship him.

   d) Being made in the image of God means that we share God's attributes of lordship.

3. (T/F) There are no common themes of morality that hold true amongst all people.

4. (T/F) Humans were given dominion over creation in the same moment that God expressed his intent to make man in his image.

5. Which of the following shows how commands for relationships are a way we are different from everything else in the created world?

   a) We display God's image through the depth of our relationships experienced with others.

   b) We display God's image when we show kindness to others.

   c) We display God's image when we acknowledge that God exists.

   d) We display God's image through adoption, birth, and the creation of family.

6. Which of the following is a way that mankind represents God?

   a) When we pave a road

   b) When we celebrate the anniversary of meeting someone

   c) When we set long-term financial goals

   d) When we worship in church

   e) All of the above

7. Every counseling need traces back to _____.

   a) Original sin

   b) A desire to repair one's relationship with God

c) A failure to fully image God
d) Conflict

8. Which New Testament term can often refer to an internal principle of indwelling sin that remains in a believer?

a) Heart
b) Flesh
c) Mind
d) Spirit

9. Christians who embrace the teaching that humanity is composed of two genders that have two different roles are called _____.

a) Egalitarians
b) Complementarians
c) Biblical counselors
d) Evangelical feminism

10. The author argues that the Bible emphasizes differences in the roles of men and women in which of the following areas?

a) Home and church
b) Biology and leadership
c) Home and marriage
d) Church and biology

CHAPTER 8

Biblical Counseling and a Theology of Sin

You Should Know

- Sin is a disposition of human beings, leads to a failure to conform to the moral law of God, a description of the bad things that humans do and fail to do, and a description of who we are as wicked people

- The timeline of sin: God created everything, and it was pronounced good; God gave a command to not eat the fruit of a certain tree; Adam and Eve disobeyed God and became sinners; spiritual separation from God for all humankind; eventual physical death for all humankind

- The seven areas of the human race that suffer the effects of sin: our standing before God, our motivations, our thinking, our emotions, our bodies, our relationships, and our world.

- In a sinful world, we experience emotions that are misplaced, wrong, and out of proportion to the occasion.

- The doctrine of total depravity means that sin has touched all elements of humanity.

- Three different contexts for counseling informed by the doctrine of sin: People seek counseling because they live life in a fallen world corrupted by sin; people seek counseling because they commit sinful acts and suffer painful consequences; people seek counseling because they are in pain from wrongs committed against them because of sin

- The only Christian response to sin in counseling: to call sinful people to repent of their sin

- The four common indicators that a counselee has engaged in biblical forgiveness: the counselee allows himself to think about the person/action that leads to a sinful emotion; the counselee brings up the sin to the person to attack that person; the counselee reveals the sin to others in order to harm them; the counselee adds unnecessary penalties to the consequences of the sin

- It is helpful to think about helping counselees to develop the <u>attitude</u> of forgiveness even when the offender's lack of confession will not allow the <u>act</u> of forgiveness to take place. (p. 312)

- The consequences of sin affect oneself, the entire existence of humanity, and the world.

Essay Questions

Short

1. Explain the Pelagian view of sin and arguments against it. Contrast this with the concept of original sin, or inherited guilt.

2. How does biblical counseling help counselees reorder emotions in a better way? (p. 222)

3. How would you go about helping a counselee address their sin through confession? Describe the two-part process of forsaking sin in your own words.

Long

1. How do you apply the principles of biblical counseling and the effects of sin on the world to help someone who is suffering pain from physical sickness? Does their sickness reflect their sin?

Quiz

1. Sin is a _____ of/for humankind.
   a) Trait
   b) Consequence

c) Disposition
d) Reality

2. How does the author describe the principle of representation in our world?

   a) Through the example of political representation and elected officials
   b) Through the example of Pelagius and the council of Carthage
   c) Through the example of the garden and God's original act of creation
   d) Through the example of school requirements and teachers

3. According to the author, which of the following does *not* refer to original sin?

   a) Adam's guilt before God is our guilt before God
   b) The first sin we commit
   c) Guilt resides in us from the beginning of our existence
   d) Adam's representation of humankind before God in his disobedience

4. Sinful behavior grows out of _____.

   a) Peer pressure to be a certain person
   b) Sinful thoughts of the human mind
   c) Sinful desires of the human heart
   d) Accusation of the conscience

5. Sin's influence on our thinking means that _____.

   a) We can be honest about the existence of God
   b) Our spiritual functions of cognition cannot be confused
   c) Biblical counseling can never truly help someone
   d) We can rationalize moral choices to make good seem bad and bad seem good

6. (T/F) Total depravity means that sin touches every aspect of our human existence and humanity as a whole with an astonishing amount of corruption.

7. Which of the following comments does Paul make about the relationships of fallen people?

   a) Our relationships are characterized by malice, envy, and animosity.
   b) Our relationships were characterized by joy, harmony, and love before the fall.
   c) Our relationships are perverted because of the fallen state of our most significant relationship.
   d) Our relationships were created to mirror that of Jesus and his disciples.

8. When people seek counseling because they live life in a fallen world, the goal of that counseling is which of the following?

   a) Help the counselee accept blame for his or her role in the painful consequences
   b) Give the counselee comfort amid the pain they are experiencing
   c) Share advice with the counselee on how to fix his or her relationship with God
   d) Direct the counselee to seek information on all the issues affecting his or her problem

9. Which of the following does *not* characterize a confession of sin?

   a) The counselee must confess recognition of his sin
   b) The counselee must confess his sin to God
   c) The counselee must confess his sin to others affected
   d) The counselee must confess with candid humility

10. Turning from sin requires _____.

   a) A humble confession of sin
   b) Forsake and stop doing the sin
   c) Put righteousness in place of the sin
   d) All of the above

CHAPTER 9

Biblical Counseling and a Theology of Suffering

You Should Know

- The six different categories of suffering discussed in the Bible: suffering brought by human sinfulness, pain caused by the world, the devil, others' pain brings painful emotions, confusion, and death

- Our own sin and the sins of others are not something we can address and leave off because sin causes painful memories and the memory of sin remains with us.

- 1 John 2:15–17 and John 15:18–19 are both examples of the world/world system type of suffering.

- "Your adversary the devil prowls around like a roaring lion, seeking someone to devour."—1 Peter 5:8 ESV

- God's Word both describes the difficulties we have and shows us how to address those difficulties.

- Trust God: the biblical counseling response to experiencing the sin of Adam in a fallen world

- God's active will: a positive demonstration of his good attributes

- God's passive will: the withdrawal of God's good attributes

- The three different categories of benefits of suffering in a sinful world: brings about spiritual fruit in our lives; helps people see the glory of God; glorifies God by maximizing our need for him

- The five realities agreed upon by Christians regarding the doctrine of last things: believers go immediately into the presence of God when they die; Jesus Christ will physically return from heaven to gather his church; all of humanity will be exposed to God's judgment on the last day; all who have not trusted in Jesus Christ will be exposed to hell's punishment; and those who trust in Jesus Christ will live with him forever in the new kingdom

Essay Questions

Short

1. How would you counsel someone suffering from sins brought about by the world system? How would you counsel someone you think may be causing suffering through the world system?

2. Explain why Jonathan Edwards' analogy of the sun helps us understand the goodness of God in a world of evil.

3. How do the five realities held by Christians regarding the doctrine of last things encourage us in the midst of suffering?

Long

1. If God is good, how can he allow the kinds of suffering we experience in this world? How can you help people also seeking answers to this question? How would you use the Bible to help a counselee encountering suffering?

Quiz

1. When the Bible talks about "the world," it means all the following except _____.
    a) The physical planet
    b) The created realm of heavens and earth
    c) The human population on the planet
    d) A mind-set of humanity that is opposed to Christ

2. The lesson of Romans 9:2–3 where Paul is experiencing painful emotions is which of the following?
   a) In a sinful world, we ought not to get involved in others' sinful behavior.
   b) The Israelites are never aware of their own sin and must be shown by others.
   c) A sinful world brings others suffering and ought to cause us pain as we have compassion.
   d) We ought to step in and take God's wrath for the sake of our brothers.

3. Which of the following is true regarding our limited knowledge?
   a) Limited knowledge is a consequence of sin .
   b) With a true desire to do right, limited knowledge is not a problem for believers.
   c) All creatures have limited knowledge.
   d) We will have complete knowledge in heaven when we are reconciled with God.

4. Biblical counseling differs from secular counseling in which of the following categories?
   a) Biblical counseling has a category for human sinfulness.
   b) Biblical counseling has a category for confusion generated by pain.
   c) Biblical counseling generates a sense of compassion for others in trouble.
   d) Secular counseling and biblical counseling have the same categories of suffering.

5. God's attributes of care are on display as he _____.
   a) Controls every event that happens in the world
   b) Directs every event that happens in the world toward good
   c) Bestows compassion and mercy toward those who are involved in every event that happens in the world
   d) Judges every event that happens in this world

6. Which of the following is an example of a primary cause?
   a) God has compassion when a cousin is diagnosed, suffers, and dies from cancer.

b) A husband struggles with pornography and allows himself to cheat on his wife.

c) God has sovereign omnipotence over terrorism.

d) The forgiveness we have in Jesus Christ when we commit sin

7. The author, Paul Helm, and Jonathan Edwards all refer to the sovereignty of God as which of the following?

a) Symmetrical

b) Asymmetrical

c) A primary cause of all events

d) An attribute of God's care

8. The teachings found in the doctrine of last things are meant to give Christians _____.

a) Justice from suffering the sins of others

b) Joy during trial

c) Comfort in God's final plan for suffering

d) Fear and awe of God's awesome power

9. Which of the following is *not* a benefit of suffering discussed in the Bible?

a) Suffering proves that we belong to Jesus

b) Suffering brings about the fruits of the Spirit in our lives

c) Suffering teaches us that we need the evil to see the good

d) Suffering helps others see the glory of God and spreads the gospel

10. Which of the following is Peter's crucial point in 1 Peter 1:6–7?

a) Our faith stands in need of testing to be genuine

b) We have a hope of our heavenly inheritance

c) We will be grieved by various trials on this earth

d) Jesus Christ is worthy of praise and glory because he gives us good things

CHAPTER 10

Biblical Counseling and a Theology of Salvation

You Should Know

- The elements in the order of salvation: election, calling, regeneration, conversion, justification, adoption, sanctification, perseverance, and glorification

- The two parts of the calling: the general call; the effective call

- Three elements of the effective call: comes from God; applies God's special grace to save in the heart of the sinner so that the words of the human minister effectively call a person to believe; it comes to individuals at a specific time; includes specific blessings to believers

- To experience conversion, a person must know something of her own sinfulness, the righteousness of Christ and his work as Savior, and God's holy character.

- As related to biblical counseling, the doctrine of salvation teaches that Christians have genuine and tangible resources to deal with problems that confront us.

- Four observations the author discusses regarding justification: justification deals with our moral standing before God; justification deals with our moral guilt through a legal declaration of righteousness; this legal declaration of forgiveness and righteousness is based on the merit of Christ; justification happens through faith

- Election: the biblical teaching that God chose from the very beginning of time those people who would ultimately come to faith in Jesus Christ

- Imputation: the process by which God applies the morality of one person to someone who did not earn it

- Sanctification: the lifelong process in which Christians strive by divine grace to grow in Christlikeness in their entire person

- Glorification: the complete perfection of believers in body and soul at the return of Jesus Christ

Essay Questions

Short

1. Explain the difference between the general call and the effective call.

2. How can God declare people to be righteous when they have so obviously sinned? How do you help counselees see the difference between God's justice system and the world's?

3. How is the doctrine of sanctification connected to the doctrines of regeneration and justification?

Long

1. Describe and summarize each of the different facets of salvation. How can you use them to teach a counselee something valuable?

Quiz

1. (T/F) Salvation is a single, one-time event that starts a process to relationship with God.

2. (T/F) Conversion marks the first, but not only, instance of faith and repentance in the life of a believer.

3. The doctrine of divine election is taught in which of the following Scriptures?

    a) Ezekiel 36:26–27

    b) Romans 9:10–21

    c) 1 Peter 2:9

    d) Hebrews 11

4. Which of the following explains the connection between election and calling?

    a) Election teaches that God determined to save people before the foundation of the world, and calling teaches that God began to call out his elect individuals at a specific time.

    b) Election teaches that God determined to save his people, and calling teaches that God does not need evangelism to bring his elect individuals to a saving knowledge with him.

    c) Election and calling are part of the same stage within the process of salvation.

    d) Election explains calling, in that election is the basis where God chooses the elect individuals who will come to a saving knowledge of him, and calling is the process for how he accomplishes this saving action through the general call of the apostles.

5. Regeneration refers to _____.

    a) The process by which the Spirit works a change of heart with the cooperation of the sinful person

    b) The dramatic change in a believer so that he has realized the fullness of his newness in Christ in the present time

    c) The sovereign and invisible work of the Spirit that transforms a believer from someone opposed to God into someone who loves God

    d) The daily process new believers need to engage in to purify all the powers of body and soul that have been defiled by original sin

6. At which stage of salvation does the first work requiring participation on the part of the elect person begin?

    a) Calling

    b) Regeneration

    c) Conversion

    d) Justification

7. Which of the following is *not* an observation of the doctrine of justification?

    a) Justification deals with our moral standing before God.

    b) Justification is given through a legal declaration of righteousness.

    c) Justification is hotly debated among Protestants and Catholics.

    d) Justification happens through repentant conversion and sincere prayer.

8. God's role in justification is which of the following?

    a) Justification is worked primarily through Jesus Christ and the Holy Spirit.

    b) God responds with a legal declaration that believers are forgiven of sin and possess his own righteousness.

    c) God keeps believers in the grace of salvation and aids them in a lifelong journey of renewal.

    d) God initiates repentant faith in the sinful person so that they turn to Jesus.

9. Which of the following is a blessing believers receive through adoption into the family of God?

    a) Common grace

    b) Election

    c) Regeneration

    d) All of the above

10. The doctrine of perseverance teaches _____.

    a) God is a faithful and loving Father who does not permit his children to be lost

b) People remain in the Christian faith regardless of any sinful attitudes and actions

c) Christians must strive to remain in God's grace and righteousness through continued right action and prayer on a lifelong journey

d) God is faithful to his children because of the doctrine of election

CHAPTER 11

Biblical Counseling and a Theology of the Church

You Should Know

- "I hope to come to you soon, but I am writing these things to you so that, if I delay, you may know how one ought to behave in the household of God, which is the church of the living God, a pillar and buttress of the truth."—1 Timothy 3:14–15

- The two realities which must take place for counseling to find a real home in the church: counseling is grounded in our understanding of the truth; the truth is rightly upheld in the context of the church

- The Bible is clear that teaching happens in a public context of preaching and in a personal context of conversation.

- Church members grow in maturity as they grow in their ability to have counseling conversations that are wise and loving.

- The four crucial ways the church can come to help a counselee: create a context for communal worship; provide fellowship; teach in the context of counseling; provide accountability

- One of the most uncomfortable situations biblical counselors face is that often the people most in need of counseling services are the people least equipped to pay for them.

- All the truths talked about here were counseled, implemented, and located in the context of the church.

- The roles of the church elder per the Bible: teaching and leading

- Parachurch ministry: a Christian faith-based organization that carries out its mission independent of church oversight

- One of the greatest assets a counselor can have: accountability to theological and methodological faithfulness in counseling

Essay Questions

Short

1. Why is understanding the doctrine of the church important in a theology of biblical counseling?

2. Can real, life-changing, God-centered change take place outside the church? Why or why not?

3. Explain how the church and biblical counselors can work together to help people with problems.

Long

1. What do you see as the role of the pastor in biblical counseling? What do you see as the role of the church community in biblical counseling?

Quiz

1. Which of the following is *not* a word used to describe the church?
    a) An organism
    b) The household of God
    c) Buttress of the truth
    d) The tree of faith

2. What approach does the author take regarding the doctrine of the church?
    a) A theological application
    b) An academic perspective

c) A practical approach
d) A controversial summary

3. Which of the following offices of the church does the author focus on?

a) Elder
b) Deacon
c) Pastor
d) Member

4. Name the two roles fulfilled by church elders.

a) Preaching and meetings
b) Preaching and home visits
c) Teaching and prayer
d) Teaching and leadership

5. The ratio of personal conversation to public preaching for Jesus in the gospels is _____.

a) 3:2
b) 5:1
c) 2:3
d) 4:1

6. Which of the following is an example of a biblical teacher that spent more time teaching in a more personal context?

a) Paul
b) Jesus
c) Moses
d) Both A & B

7. Which of the following passages clearly instructs pastors to exercise leadership to help the church counsel others?

a) 1 Timothy 3:2
b) Romans 12:1
c) Ephesians 4:15
d) Titus 1:9

8. Which of the following is *not* a role of the church community in counseling?

   a) Give discipline and care
   b) Illustrate God's judgment
   c) Create a context for worship
   d) Provide accountability

9. A parachurch ministry refers to _____.

   a) A ministry program within the church that does not specifically focus on preaching and teaching or worship
   b) A Christian faith-based ministry that used to be a church but has changed its mission to better serve the local community in other ways
   c) A Christian faith-based organization that carries out its mission independent of church oversight
   d) A religious organization that has ties to a local church and is under its authority

10. Locating counselees in community groups in faithful local churches is an effective way to do which of the following?

   a) Connect the counselee with solid and helpful relationships and teachings that work with the goals of counseling
   b) Connect the counselee to a community that can continue the counseling process alone
   c) Show the counselee what it looks like to be worshipping, healed, forgiven, and free of their issues
   d) Bring the counselee into a more trusting relationship with others in their community

ANSWER KEY

1. D, 2. C, 3. A, 4. D, 5. B, 6. D, 7. C, 8. B, 9. C, 10. A

CHAPTER 12

Biblical Counseling and the Goal of Theology

You Should Know

- A theological foundation for counseling exists regardless of whether individual practitioners know it exists, whether their foundation is right or wrong, whether their foundation is helpful or unhelpful.

- Two key ways the author uses to describe the relationship between theology and counseling: a demonstration of how particular doctrines uphold the counseling task; the experience of pregnancy for a couple

- The very process of pregnancy requires you to recognize that every new and exciting discovery points to the longing of all loving parents to see their baby in person.

- The categories of information gleaned during both pregnancy and a study of theology: general knowledge (development, science, facts); personal knowledge (baby's heartbeat, seeing a face on an ultrasound, experiences of God in one's personal life)

- The culmination of a study of theology is superior to the knowledge of that information.

- The culmination of theological knowledge: to know Christ and have a relationship with him; ministry, to point others to God

- "Indeed, I count everything as loss because of the surpassing worth of knowing Christ Jesus my Lord."—Philippians 3:8

- For Paul, the goal of theological knowledge was knowing Jesus Christ.

- Examples of the theological knowledge Paul used to write the letter to the Philippians: justification, doctrine of God, doctrine of Christ, sin and suffering, perseverance

- One of the most significant aspirations of theology is counseling.

Essay Questions

Short

1. The author gives two ways of describing the relationship between theology and counseling—through doctrines in action and through the experience of pregnancy for a couple. Which do you identify with more and why?

2. Do you agree with the author's two answers as to what the culmination of theological knowledge is? Why or why not?

3. How does Paul take theology and turn it into ministry? How can you do the same as a biblical counselor?

Long

1. Describe the relationship between theology and counseling. How might an unsound theological foundation affect one's perspective on biblical counseling? Give some examples.

Quiz

1. According to the author, what kind of connection exists between theology and counseling?
    a) There is no connection between them.
    b) There is an inseparable connection between them.
    c) There is sometimes a connection between them.
    d) There is a one-way connection between them.

2. (T/F) The theological foundation for counseling exists only whether individual practitioners have a helpful and correct foundation in God's Word.

3. (T/F) The only way to show a solid theological foundation for biblical counseling is to illustrate practical applications of doctrines upheld by the church.

4. Which of the following explains why the author and his wife were discontent as their pregnancy moved toward completion?
   a) They were fearful of what God was doing in their lives.
   b) They were in awe of what God was doing in their lives.
   c) The information they were reading in preparation for the birth only stoked anticipation to experience life with their child.
   d) The information they were reading in preparation for the birth did not correspond to getting to see their child in person.

5. Which of the following was not a step toward culmination of life together after pregnancy?
   a) Gathering knowledge
   b) Prayer
   c) Anticipation
   d) Blame

6. (T/F) It would be wrong to live content with knowledge of God but desiring no experience of him.

7. (T/F) The only real issue for counselors is whether his or her theology is faithful or faithless.

8. Which of the following is an answer given by the author to the culmination of theological knowledge?
   a) We study theology so we can know Christ and have a relationship with him.
   b) We study theology so we can be good biblical counselors.
   c) We study theology so we will truly fulfill the role of the church.
   d) We study theology so we point others to come visit a church.

9. In Philippians, Paul's goal for theological knowledge is _____.

a) Theological knowledge
b) Growth of the church
c) Knowing Jesus Christ
d) Dying for Christ

10. In Philippians, Paul uses theological knowledge to _____.

a) Know Jesus Christ
b) Point others to Christ
c) Earn salvation
d) Live a successful life

Notes

www.ingramcontent.com/pod-product-compliance
Lightning Source LLC
Chambersburg PA
CBHW010921040426
42445CB00017B/1937